CATSS
BY
GROSS

S. Gross

Ballantine Books 🐾 **New York**

All rights reserved under International and Pan-American Copyright Conventions. Published in the United States by Ballantine Books, a division of Random House, Inc., New York, and simultaneously in Canada by Random House of Canada, Limited, Toronto.

Grateful acknowledgment is made to *The New Yorker* for permission to reprint cartoons which, as indicated throughout the book, originally appeared in that magazine.

Some of the cartoons in this collection have appeared in the following books and periodicals: *Audubon, Cats Cats Cats, Cat Cartoon-a-Day Calendar, Cosmopolitan, Good Housekeeping, Harvard Business Review, National Lampoon, OBG Management,* and *TV Guide.*

Library of Congress Catalog Card Number: 94-94636

ISBN: 0-345-39277-9

Cover design by Georgia Morrissey

Manufactured in the United States of America

First Edition: April 1995

10 9 8 7 6 5 4 3 2 1

"*What kind of mischief are you into now?*"

"If we were lawyers, this would be billable time."

"Get down from there!"

"They're all mysterious, but this one especially so."

S. GROSS

"That's the dog star. There is no cat star."

"We don't have a kitty heaven up here. What I can do, though, is reincarnate you as a cocker spaniel and if you're real good, you'll have a shot at doggie heaven when you die again."

S. GROSS

S.GROSS

"It's not a bad job, Willie, except I'm being stalked by a cat."

"I'm the muse of cat books."

"First of all, Miss Havermayer, I would like to express my condolences on your loss. Secondly, if you read the fine print, you would see that there are no monies due. The first two lives are deductible."

S. GROSS

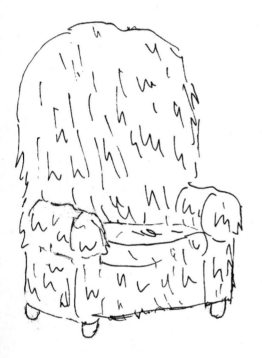

S.GROSS

"Hey, there's nothing to read here but cat books!"

"But honey, cats are supposed to shed."

"You got the cat all hot and bothered."

S. GROSS

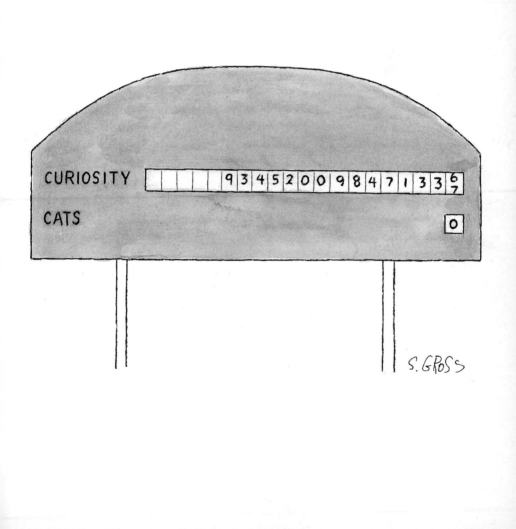

"I don't like having birds on my back."

S. GROSS

"Would you please rise? He thinks he's the king of the cats and we play along."

"*I'm thinking of having her declawed.*"

S.GROSS

"My, my. The cat show has gotten quite whimsical this year."

24 HOUR
TUNA

S. GROSS

S. GROSS

"Thank you. You've been a great audience."

"Now you know why I hate cats."

S. GROSS

"It's the legs that go first."

"Don't think I don't know that you're sitting there plotting ways
to make me get rid of my cat!"

S. GROSS

"Too late! The meter ran out. You get a cat."

"Maybe he's not getting enough iron."

"It's ten o'clock. Do you know where your squeaky toy is?"

ON THE EIGHTH DAY GOD CREATED CATS

S.GROSS

"It's a fur ball. Quick, give her the Heimlich maneuver."

"Be still! The world needs more pussycats on velvet!"

"Dogs play poker. Cats play solitaire."

S.GROSS

"Let's face it, JoJo, you're just not a cat person."

"We could be living a lot better if you didn't have to pay alimony to that goddamn pussycat!"

"I'm going out. Do you need any voles?"

S.GROSS

"Cats! You can't live with them and you can't live without them."

"It's chicken and tuna, sweetie."

"We're saved! It's tuna fish in water!"

S.GROSS

"It still hasn't let up out there, so I guess I'll have another one."

S. GROSS

"Is this your idea of bathroom humor?"

S. GROSS

"The 'all clear' has sounded."

"I got rid of the bird smell."

"Getting talked into wearing a bell is one thing,
but who suckered you into stereo?"

"With every anchovy pizza ordered, you get a free cat."

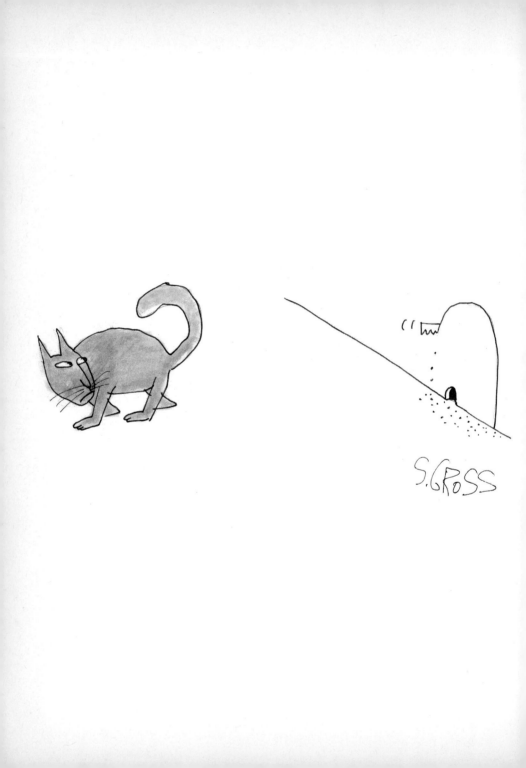

"Must you take along your damn cat?"

"*Don't eat the plants.*"

Cats are not as intelligent as you think.

"*Before I get spayed, I'd like a second opinion.*"

S. GROSS

"The cat told me to eat your homework."

"They're cat trading cards."

S.GROSS

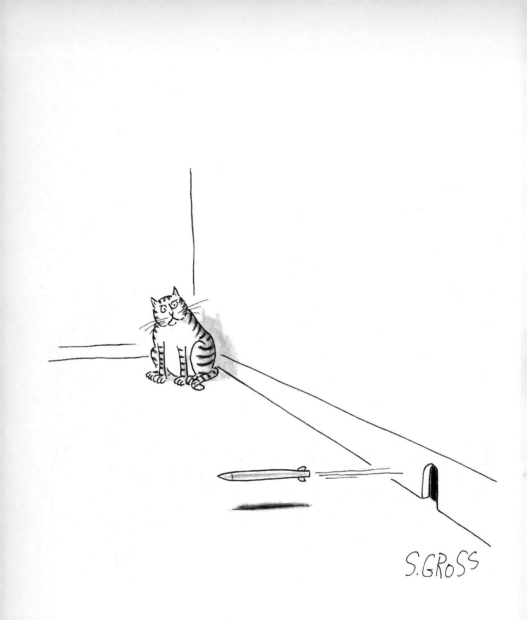

"That's my cat. Her name is Pumpkin."

"What happened to the blackbirds?"

S. GROSS

"Ten lives."

S.GROSS

ABOUT THE AUTHOR

S. GROSS was raised by wolves in the Carpathian Mountains of Eastern Europe. He saw his first cat at age twelve when his mother chased one up a tree. For the next ten years he watched various relatives chase cats up trees—and other high places; while the animals were up there, he started sketching them. These sketches evolved into cartoons—and after he was trapped and taught to read by an order of Trappist nuns, he put captions under some of them (the cartoons, not the nuns). Mr. Gross hopes you enjoy the drawings and he wishes to thank his mother for making this book possible.